You are loved

by Zahabiya Quraishi

Dedication

For my daughter Hana, and for every
girl around the world.

Hana loved to be amongst nature.

Whenever Hana wanted to think or have a break, she perched beneath the giant oak tree in her garden.

She spent many moments under that oak tree in her garden.

Hana had a bad day today. She was fed up.

Some things did not go the way she wanted.

She missed her school alarm. She forgot her lunch.

And she also tripped on a stone on the way back from school.

As soon as she came home, she knew she wanted to go outside. So she got out of her school uniform, put on her favourite polka dot hijab, ran past the colourful flowers and headed straight to the oak tree in the garden.

She stood in front of the oak tree and was about to sit when she saw something shining on the body of the tree trunk!

As she got closer, she carefully wiped away the dust and debris and revealed a glistening mirror.

She squinted her
eyes and could barely
recognise herself. It had
been a long time since
she had looked in a
mirror.

"I'm so ugly!" exclaimed Hana.
She started sobbing lightly under the
oak tree. Then her mother noticed.
Hana, what's the matter?" said her
mother.
"I'm not beautiful, Mum," sobbed Hana.
"That's not true, honey," said Mum.

"You are: "Bright. Bright like the sun. Allah SWT gave it so much light, and it serves the whole of mankind.

"Strong like an oak tree, as Allah SWT gave it roots full of strength and the ability to stand tall.

"Beautiful like a flower, as Allah SWT blessed it with colour and perfumed it with fragrance.

"Creative like a spider. Allah SWT allowed it to build amazing webs from silk in different shapes and sizes.

"Confident like a bird who goes out to find food every day. The bird puts his trust in Allah SWT, and Allah SWT provides for him.

"Unique, like a leaf. Allah SWT made leaves in a variety of shapes, colours and sizes. Not one is the same as another.

"And most of all, you are loved . . . you are loved by the most loving,
Allah SWT. And loved by your family and friends."

Printed in Great Britain
by Amazon

42203496R00016